DE HOMEPLACE
Poems for Renewal
by
Young People of Caribbean Origin

Edited by
ABDUL MALIK

Financially assisted by the **Inner London Education Authority**

Published by PANRUN COLLECTIVE 1990

Copyright © Panrun Collective

Cover design by Wascilla

Typeset and printed by RAP Ltd, 201 Spotland Road, Rochdale OL12 7AF

ISBN 0 9513173 1 8

Panrun Collective exists to promote the work of Caribbean artists (poets, performers of poetry and other creative writers) through publishing, recording, teaching, lecturing and organising performances.

Panrun Collective
46A Trent Road
Brixton
London SW2 5BL
Tel: 071 274 3292

Specially dedicated to the Course of Education

Special thanks to Foufou and members of the Collective for all their hard work.

Contents

Introduction

Time-Year

Panrun Collective is an England based non-profit-making organisation made up of poets, performers, writers and educationists. We began functioning in 1987. This is our third project in keeping with our "Breaking New Ground" commitment: an anthology of previously unpublished poems written by twenty-five year olds and under, living in the Caribbean; and of Caribbean descent living in Britain, Germany, Canada and North America. The projected themes were: Identity, Transmigration, Social Conflict and Love.

We wish to thank the following organisations for their promotional support in this successfully concluded venture:- New Voices Poetry Magazine (Trinidad), Groundwork Theatre Company (Jamaica), The Caribbean Times (Britain), The Voice (Britain), The Daily Gleaner (Jamaica), Lambeth Library (Britain), Caribbean Contact, Gayelle (Trinidad), Castries Library (St. Lucia), The Chronicle (Guyana), Antilla (Martinique), The Dominica Writers' Guild (Dominica), Stabroek News (Guyana), Chelmsford County Library (Britain), Culture Word Information Bulletin (Britain), Artrage (Britain), and individual teachers in schools and colleges throughout Britain and the Caribbean.

Public response was indeed phenomenal, reaching almost overwhelming proportions here in England. And the compilation period of poems was from September 1988 to September 1989. Panrun Collective therefore takes special pride in delivering this thematically appealing and anxiously awaited work, with the momentum of its gestation '88 — '89 — with the underpinning momentum of Eastern European upheavals '89 — '90 ... in the time-year of the Horse (of China) — in the time-year of 'discrediting' SOCIALISM — in the time-year of dismantling STALINISM

— in the time-year marking the release of NELSON
MANDELA — in the time-year marking the TWENTY-FIFTH
anniversary of the assassination of MALCOLM X ...

So occasioned, DE HOMEPLACE offers timely and crucial
testimony of our own state(s) within the Western
Capitalist Block — of our own dilemma-driven HUMANITY
as perceived by a new fast-forwarding generation ... a
spinning-between-THIRD-and-FIRST-WORLDs-generation ...
a now-in-the-throes-of-their-own-comeuppance-generation
... a generation moulded by the Cultural renaissance of the
Caribbean — the new poetry of the '70s and '80s. .. a
generation resplendent and embracing, refracted in the
dual light of LANGUAGE and LIBERATION ... So graced,
DE HOMEPLACE moves beyond shallow sloganeering —
beyond subjective poetical attachment — beyond
beckoning island nostalgia ... to being a rallying cri de
coeur for cohesion, for renewal, within the diaspora —
within our own state(s) of advanced displacement ... so
paced, DE HOMEPLACE becomes an inherently promising,
highly spirited and purposeful work for the momentum of
the Nineties ... for 1992, the commemorative time-year of
Columbus's 'discovery' of America and the New World ...
for 1992, the projected time-year of the new European
Economic 'Unity' ... THOSE THAT HAVE EYES TO SEE
LET THEM SEE AND EARS TO HEAR LET THEM HEAR ...

A new generation speaks with new urgency to be seen, to
be heard, to be understood — in this time-year of the final
decade, this time-year count down to the Twenty-first
century.

D.A.M.D.
Delano Abdul Malik De Coteau

Le Lambi

Vent du loin
Vent du large
La conque du rivage
Garde les souvenirs
Des continents altérés
Et murmure à nos oreilles
La triste mélodie des océans.
Le lambi cache au fond de lui
Des secrets enfouis
Et ranime le chant
Des peuples ébranlés.

Allix Belrose-Huyghues
Germany/Guadeloupe/Martinique

The Lambi Shell

Wind from afar
Wind from the sea ...
This shell from the shore
Guards memories
Of altered continents,
And murmurs in our ears
The sad melody of oceans.
This conch shell hides in its depths
Suppressed secrets
And brings to life again
The story of scattered peoples.

CALL

Khem 6000

KHEM land of wonderblack and golden sands
colossal ikons and enchanted temples.
An ancient mystery
of religion science and magic
BLACK BLAck BLack Black magic
BLACK BLAck BLack Black people.
Child of the burnt faces
mother of civilisation reveal yourself.

Your seed arose on the bank of the Nile
and stretched across the world of mortal men.
Head of man body of dog
worshippers of the Sun god
Light of life Light of this world
Amon RA Amon RA Amon RA

Nocturnal bodies covered by your light
golden shine of the sand so bright
Elevated to gods of time and place
Osiris Isis Horus reveal your black faces

Revered in glory spread in history
to worlds both old and new
to cultures both false and true
Do you know who?
Do you know who you are?

From near from afar

Rivers of visions
space of race
Dreams of life out there out there
back here back here

From the North the North the North
cold enemies came forth
Barren desert blades
who came to invade enslave degrade and persuade
Nocturnal star stroked people

From the North the North the North

Kenrick Courtney Whitaker
Britain

Mask

After they
invaded our land
stole our masks
and broke our gods
I had no face to speak
to seek god in I self
was fear
of that dark hull:
(some of us were able to smuggle our gods
inside the belly of our dreams)

in new land
long frocked christ people
blessed the place
where shackles burnt
teaching tolerance
making criss cross sign
on their naked breast
these dumb oracles had no masks

ear learnt this dumb tongue
until back
could break no more
then independence
incubated in those dark hulls
hatched in the belly of our minds
we tried to raise our gods
dance shango but

our masks
were locked in a tomb
in their museum

now poem must become mask
pull us from the belly
of our dreams
unshackle tongue
to sing eye song and
dance freedom in the streets
for I self
and the children

the will is everything
they can not
break our gods again

Hugh Stultz
Britain/Jamaica

Sister Brother I

Black as the night shawl
to wrap around the early hours of your first dawn.

Black as the mothering arms that hold you.
Black as the delicate fingers that cajole you.

Black as the bejewelled earth
Black as century-old stories
that tell of your ancestral worth.

Black
You are Sheba's daughters
Black your souls bathed in African waters.

Black are the tender faces that shine before me
A myriad of possibilities

Black like you
And me.

Dawn Burgess
Britain

Abiku

Abiku is a stubborn child
the child of sinners
the child of saints
his world is the dead
his door the womb

Abiku's laughter echoes
in the closets of the mind
where sleep hides and husbands cry
when friends fall over
their own unbelief

Abiku's roots are planted in darkness
why else would he shun
his mother's smile

Woman when your labour is pain
Abiku will snatch the hope from your eye
write poison on the womb
    'I am a dead child
    your womb is my grave
    I seek another grave to lie
    another mind to crucify
    you will not smile, woman
    they will not call you mother
    I am a dead-born
    I am a dead-born'

Hugh Stultz
Britain/Jamaica

Remnants of Time

Erase old dances,
old songs, old
Trinity
Marred by western ideals
Sad eh?
It real sad boy...

Pitch turns to ash
with the glare of
indifference to
melodious sunsets
Ravaged
Spewed from Columbus' womb
Like a birth?
More like death to me

Shake the coconut trees
Play the pan
Walk over footprints left on
firm sand
Smooth pebbles are hot coal
We dance

Untouched pillars awake
To sweet cacophany
Rhythmic gems
titillate, vibrate Trinity's peaks
In amber cedar groves
In Laventille?

Drum beats night after night
Jewels create
sweet music
steel pan they say
wakes the dead panmen
Awake, arise
Get up
Dance

Lagahou, douen, Papa Bois
Shake the chac-chac
Beat the bongo drum
In forest wave
flow over the new wave
Lost soul, lost land....

Dawn Mahailia Riley
Trinidad and Tobago

We

It is hard to write of sun and sea
when the spirits of people locked within me
find garbled expression,
       Sounding unformed
       rise
       now, rise
       then, the drums!
       The drums I hear!
       Music I feel fight!
       (rhythm quickened)
       (stringed crescendo)
       Struggle! Crash!
       Souls cry out, crush
       me
       Mercy! Mercy!
Sitar not congo
congo not sitar or guitar which
one plays?
       Pa-ma, I hear your voices
       sounding, drumming, ancient
       passions bounding
Cannot choose
       I grasp,
            grip, lose
Tormented: expression fails.

Great-great man-woman-child who childed me
Cultures warped and weft, warbled
tongues and thinking, secrets
buried in soil, shielded
by sugar and rice, mute.

                          Paloma Mohamed.
                          Guyana

Rastafari

I awoke one morning with a burning need
a need to feed
Hunger for the meaning of my life love and death
from the day we are born we await our dying breath
I must know to be sure
then I heard the beating drum the beat so pure
As a moth to the light I was drawn
it would reveal all
beckoning I towards the fire was the riddim call

　　　You are not alone
　　　Africa is your home
　　　You are not alone
　　　I&I is one

I is a family a tribe a nation inna irration
Don't let others speak on your behalf
decide your destination
　　　Your blood is red
　　　Your soul is gold
　　　Your land is green
Your locks are the sign that mark you free
Persecuted for your strength
that is the curse that knowledge brings
but have faith my people
for you walk in the wake of the conquering Lion of Judah
THE KING OF KINGS
I tell you your name is a lie
you are the son of JAH RASTAFARI.

Colin Benjamin
Britain

Roll Call

From a pickney I check for the Ska and Rock Steady
Scratch, Aitken, Wailers, Maytals and Dekker
Then I reach five and step outside
I listen to the charts — Glitter Band, BCR, Darts
The years in between with culture so lean
I man a check all the New Wave Music
In 1981 to the reggae fold I return
Sponji Reggae made I soul BURN
From '81 to '83 I check for the radical rockers reggae
In 1984 I start as sound selector
In 1985 Wee Yellow Rip a dub it live
In 1986 I had to take up the sticks
In 1987 Ambassadors rule with Dancehall riddims
supporting Dennis Brown — prophet & Prince
In 1988 through movements I take a break
In 1989 I have to lay it on the line
Cos 1990 is the time when the lyrics a rhyme
Coming out furious cleansing my mind
They'll want to stop, change, blackmail me
But I stand fine burn — a Black male already.

Karl Duff
Britain

The Army

Me chanting pun de mike mi chat it personally
A personal appearance from a classic M.C.
In ranking I'm the boss and not the secretary,
Im on dis microphone to chat about di army,
To anyone who's thinking of joining the army,
The RAF THE PARATROOPERS OR THE NAVY;
Tek that idea out of your head I would advise you
strongly,
You'll see exactly what I mean when I tell you this story.

Mi friend a go ina the army
Mi friend a go ina the armEEEEEE
Im say im going in the army,
Because it's good ina di army

                    Hear weh him say

Dem give you proper shelter and dem pay you money,
Dem rank you as a private and dem pay you weekly,
You geta army clothes and a smart red beret,
And a black pair of boots that are very shiny
You're working for your queen and you can serve your
country,
You get promote by the queen fi any great bravery,
And if the deed that you done was done very bravely,
You could of earn a coupla stripes or could
even earn 3.

Him say him going in the army,
Mi say no go ina no armeee,
It's a bad life in the army,
don't even think about no army,

                    I tell him why

Dem tekway you name and you identity
You have to wake up every morning at 5.30
You always a work it's like damn slavery

You only get ten day to go and see your family,
You can't go no blues you can't go no party
You can't get noh splif, you can't get no sensi
Di camp full up a man you won't see a lady.

No go ina no army,
him say, "You just a try fi scare me,
It's a good life ina di army"
Den him a start fi argue with me.

Hear weh we say

him You look smart on parade with you red beret hat
me but if you tilt your hat a bit wrong would a get a hard
     slap
him you learn to read a compass you learn to read a map
me dem things are so confusen, they will turn you idiot
him dem build up your muscles with a heavy rucksack,
me dem ting deh are so heavy they will brok up your back
him you live in the barracks that's a change from a flat
me mi say it's damp, it's smelly, it's full up of rat
him dem mek you fatter if you're skinny, rnek you fitter if
     you're fat
me But if you see the food they give you, you'd not be
     saying that
         dem mek it like you're on some kind of diet
me the food, it wouldn't fill up the belly of a rat
me dem call you Paki if you're Asian, call you Nigger if
     you're black
me join the army if I was you I would not do that

Den him say

Maybe the army was not such a good choice
In the army it's not very nice
I think I might just take your advice
In fact, g'way with the army just to be quite precise.

Ian Brighton
Britain

Image

Caribéenne

Interprétation sur la
"Récolte des Fruits en Martinique" de P. Gaugin.

Debout le bras tendu
  Courbée les mains au sol.
    Droite avec ton panier
      Dressé sur la tête.
        Assise dégustant un corossol
          Vetue de blanc de vert de bleu
            Coiffée d'un madras ou d'un bacoua.
          Fichu sur les épaules
            La taille marée

            Le regard en avant
              Fixant le passé
                Saisissant l'avenir
                  Tu es de tous ces noms
                    Noire métisse mulatresse
                    Chabine coolie capresse
                    Zambo goyave chapée
                    Tu en as fait une nation.
                    Je t'écoute sur la véranda
                    Donner la formule magique
                    Du "Krik ... Krak..."
                    De nos légendes.

                    Noire métisse mûlatresse
                    Chabine coolie câpresse
                    Zambo goyave chapée békée
                    Qu'importe tous ces noms
                    Je ne sens que ton âme
                    Riche de tous ces parfums
                    Puisqu'elle m'est familière
                    Comme la terre Caraïbe.

Allix Belrose-Huyghues
Germany/Martinique//Guadeloupe

Caribbean Woman

Meditation on Gaugin's painting
'Fruit Gathering in Martinique'.

Erect, your arm extended
  Bent down, your hands to earth ...
    Upright with your basket
      Balanced on your head.
        Scented, savouring a soursop...
          Dressed in white/green/blue
            Hair wrapped in silk or cotton scarf
            Shawl on shoulders
            Waist sashed.

          Looking ahead
            Fixing the past
              Seizing the future
                You are made up of all these names:
                Black Mixed-race Mulato
                  Shabine Coolie Goat-girl
                  Sambo Guava Run-away ...
                    You've made a nation of them.
                    I hear you on the veranda
                    Utter the magic spell
                      The "Crick ... Crack"
                      Of our tales.

            Black Mixed-race Mulato
              Shabine Coolie Goat-girl
                Sambo Guava Run-away Békée.
                What does it matter, all these
                  names?
                I only sense your soul
                  Rich with all these scents
                    Because it's as familiar to me
                    As the Caribbean earth.

Allix Belrose-Huyghues
Germany/Guadeloupe/Martinique

17

Far Cry

I wouldn't mind if I were from Pakistan,
But I wasn't, But the word 'Paki' became my all.
The music of the sitar,
Tales of the greatness of Allah,
All the shalwal and orni
A hundred years of toil in muddy paddy-fields,
All compressed in to one word 'Paki'.

Wouldn't they like to know that I am a descendant
of Mohammed the greatest prophet.
That I can say 'Assalaam-Au-Alaikum' and
not stutter.
Also that I found their country beautiful and
worthy of the blessings of Allah, or is it their
Allah now?
To them I have no compassion, no beliefs.

Is it thinking, about PAKI and ABDULLAH,
If they would just say 'ABI' it would be ....
'Hey Paki'.
No Answer.
'Hey Paki I'm talkin' to you.'
'Listen Americani I don't like you calling me
Paki, so don't.'
'OK so what's your name Paki?'
To them I am nothing.

Heidi Holder
Trinidad and Tobago

Confusion

The Sky is dark and angry,
The wind is rustling through the weary leaves,
All the elements seem to be threatening me,
Where do I fit in?

I am struggling in the midst of a hurricane,
Fighting like the trees for balance and peace,
Should I dance to the music of the wind
Or continue to be an outcast, disjointed.

There is no in-between, I can dance
or continue to search for inner peace, until I die.
I must be in control of myself
for my every motion carves my destiny.

Carlene Hall
Trinidad and Tobago

Yam Man

The first Yam-Son
the second Yam-Son,
And a third.
      '...dem saying he'an Englishman...'
But he is saying
     'I am a British-man.'

And here I stand,
Black.
A Britain.
A quiet man
But not quite the Gentle-man.

And here I stand,
Separated from the Yam-Man,
     (my father)
By NOTHING
'cept time.

There He stands.
Enjoying the small rewards
which once,
as dreams,
seemed worth so much more.
Travelling two thousand miles
to reap,
to keep,
Not to swap!

The Yam-Man
The Yam-Son
Dream on.

Oh my England!

And now we both stand,
Flumuxed, Guzumped.
Staring hard in disbelief
        First to each other,
And then
        To the rough ocean
Which we believed
would placate
when crossed.

Placing his hand
upon my back
He revealed to me
the product of
A Century of dreams.

His shoulders,
My shoulders,
Black soldiers.

Strong back,
arched and ready
to take all the pain
Inflicted again,
and again
AND AGAIN!

Spencer Louis Shorte
Britain

Credit Where Credit's Due

Credit where credit's due.
     (For if your earning potential is
     so great you do indeed deserve credit).
And for good measure let's throw in
Lack of interest.

Credit where credit's due.
Hallelu...
     The man who approved my loan
     at the bank in the High Street
     was black.
...jah!

Credit where credit's due.
Hallelu...
     But why did I rejoice?
     For he was a man
     with a mind and
     ambition.
     Stature befitting
     a position of respect.
...JAH!

Yes they are there,
all around;
Black.
Lawyers, managers, doctors and teachers;
Murderers, rapists, and
and even some shopkeepers.
By all accounts a normal population
Dispersed amongst a normal situation.

I will not draw your suspense.
I will tell you
why in the presence of a black financial wizard
I swelled with self respect.

It's simple.

You see...
He will KNOW,
with his finger on the city's pulse,
portfolio and his Filo-Hoax,
That Credit for us Black folk
is credit given only where it is due.

Thank You.

You See...
He knows (Having studied contractual
    obligation carefully)
He knows what value we have.

Below lies the truth.
The gesture of goodwill.
The latent catch in the tiny print...

'Credit where credit's due.

Credit is yours to spend as you will,
Bound by a signature, expenditure,
and bill.
        But don't expect a handshake,
for it's a universal truth,
that your presence is worth tuppence
and so your spending limit's TWO.'

Spencer Louis Shorte
Britain

23

Black Man

Green tweed jacket, beige trousers
thick English accent,
with every syllable properly pronounced,
Black Man.

Wide knowledge of European history,
Columbus' travels, 'English Enterprise'
Progress in Russia
Black Man.

Straight back, stiffwalk, stiff
upper lip (with lips pushed in)
Black Man.

Technical poetry that makes you
think nonsense, with intricately
linked words, hollow in essence
Black Man.

Birdmusic floating lithely through
the air
Murderous twisted yells of heavy rock
Beatless Beat
Black Man.

You've sold the mirror of your
soul
White Man.

Rosalie Joseph
Britain

Cultural Shock

In advent ...
My mind,
Dominated by confusion.
My personality,
Suffering temporary losses.
In the immersion,
Of
The cultural mosaic.

Living ...
In myself.
Trying ... to analyse ...
This society,
To understand,
Its norms, beliefs, values.

'ANOTHER LIFE'
Derek Walcott would call it,
Politically,
Socially,
Economically.

Emanating out of myself,
Apprehending the culture,
Metamorphosis halted.

Carleen T. Jules
Canada/St. Lucia

A Photo, please!

If you say God
Is Black
They tell you that's
Blasphemy

If you say God
Is Yellow
They tell you that's
Lying

If you say God
Is Brown
They tell you that's
Ignorance

But if you say,
Yes if you say God
Is white
They say
God is white.

Amanda Juliet Appiah
Britain

Didn't Want to Spoil Me

I remember quite clearly
Television on
The window where
Monty and I had played for hours

Sitting around the table
Dad and I
He
At the head of the table
Me
In my place

Struggling
It's tuff
Natty, coarse and thick
And I couldn't comb it

'I wish I was white'
I could feel I was being watched
I looked up
Pops was already looking

I didn't feel no way
But looking back at that expression
He did
I returned to my task

He leaned back in his chair
Bit his lip for the next race
'Come on bwoy, Come on bwoy'

Discipline from that day
Was much more severe

Jay A James
Britain

Image

Her hair, a black silk curtain;
Iron-pressed, washed, iron pressed,
Her silky mane
Envy of all her friends
Her elf-like beauty
Her sleek, slim lithe body
Entrances all the men
Until the dream fades away ...

Amanda Juliet Appiah
Britain

Revealing Eyes

Feelings of hurt,
I feel ... I feel ...
Feelings of despair,
I know, I know,
Feelings of guilt,
I experience so many times
Why can't these feelings go?

Pent up inside, waiting to overflow,
So deep inside ... inside ...
No one understands the pain I feel,
Does anyone really try?

Feelings of despair,
I feel ... I feel ...
When would it ever end?
Maybe it's a cycle or even a circle?
Circles have no end.

Feelings I feel,
Feelings I hide,
So deep inside my realm,
My only give-away, my only display,
My eyes ... my eyes ... my eyes ...

Carolyn Gloudon
U.S.A./Trinidad and Tobago

When I Get Outta Here

We come to Britain
They took a house down the road

Man de fight in those days

It was all a bit much for her
She worked hard for what she's got
Even now
She deh ah hospikal
In and out ... In and out
She see the children from time to time
De husban
'im naw lef er
Him deh wid one white gyal
Dem seh dats what drive er
But me ...
Me naw feel soh
I come in from work
Cook some food
To tek for her
Bwoy, she mek me laugh yuh see

'Dese people in here
Tell ME say I am mad
From the day my granny said to me

Is what yuh teking yuh pretty white shirt for
Dem naw have naw sun out deh fe dry it

I should ah in know
Said
Is madness I was coming to
She died ... last year

Me colour just lef me

Bwoy when I get outta here ...

De people in here ... DEM MAD
Look pan dat woman over deh
An dem seh
ME MAD
When I get outta here
Is home I going
Den I can wear me pretty white shirt
Me ever show it to yuh
You will like it'

While she is talking
She takes the tablets them give her
An stuffs them into the cushion she is making

'When I leave
I will leave this cushion for de nurses'

An she smile
Bwoy, dat woman can give yuh some joke yuh see

Jay A. James
Britain

When I Get Home

Awakening to the smile of a friendly face,
I was issued instructions to which I complied.
I stare out the window at the scene below;
Its diminutive appearance, beautiful,
And fascinating like a velvet carpet.
I remember the place I once was a part;
Majestic Pitons, the breath-taking scene
Of the Sulphur Springs.

— The historical aspect of Caribs and Arawaks,
To captivating flamboyance of La Rose,
Form the richness of my native culture. —

The waves cascading upon the reefs,
The shingle following the crescent waves.
This is the place where I belong;
The land, the people,
My beautiful island home.

Wayne Arthur
St. Lucia

PLACE

De Homeplace

De same sun
but different rays,
royal red-yellow rich rays
shining and burning we dark skin,
tanning we more and laughing with we
like only de sun could laugh.

De same sun
but different rays,
bright, brilliant, burning rays
on we swaying trees,
on we smiling, singing, sweet smelling streets
on we de happy, sad, guilt-free street people;

Some leave and we laugh
'More for We.'
Dis Island have eyes
large, dark-brown ones
and when they glow
is we moon,
their welcome tears does full up we sea.

Bonnie Peters
Trinidad and Tobago

Coloured Mirages

A yellow moon
With a scarred face
Casts a blue shadow
On a litter-strewn pavement
Big black monstrosities
Stand tall
Reflecting their images
On a deserted highway
Three miles away
A white moon
With a clear complexion
Sleeps upon the shores
Of a spent ocean
With one eye open
The other one blind
High up on a rocky cliff
Sits a silhouetted figure
A black woman

The cold wind
Lashes out at her
Wrapping around her emotions
Above her; a red sky
Is a blanket of the
                    Hate,
                        Distrust,
                                Disappointment
She has known
It hovers over her head
Below her, the blue sea
Is a blanket of
                    Love,
                        Healing,
                                Happiness

Descending into the ocean
Like a poem with no words
Life has no hope
A black woman
In the blue moonlight
A black woman
Who won't see the sun tomorrow.

Yvette Regis
St. Lucia

Guadeloupe Au Fond Du Coeur

La Guadeloupe
  Papillon
  Papillon grêle
  Papillon qui bat de l'aile.

La Guadeloupe
  Jeune
  Jeune abeille
  Jeune qui lutte pour sa place au soleil.

La Guadeloupe
  Cherche
  Cherche son moi
  Cherche qui lui rendra sa voie.

La Guadeloupe
  Angoisse
  Angoisse nocturne
  Angoisse qui sévit meme avec la lune.

La Guadeloupe
  Objet
  Objet sursitaire
  Objet qui gémit entre le marteau et l'enclume de fer.

La Guadeloupe
  Chaise
  Chaise à porteurs
  Chaise qui croule sous le poids des passants.

La Guadeloupe
  Pierre
  Pierre angulaire
  Pierre qui soutient l'édifice séculaire.

La Guadeloupe
   Cheval
   Cheval de mer
   Cheval qui lutte pour atteindre la terre.

La Guadeloupe
   Messagère
   Messagère du soir
   Messagère qui apporte l'espoir.

La Guadeloupe
   Bonne
   Bonne aventure
   Bonne qui raconte des vertes et des pas mûres.

Jean Juraver
Guadeloupe

Guadeloupe Deep in my Heart

Guadeloupe
Butterfly
Delicate butterfly
Butterfly fluttering its wings.

Guadeloupe
Young one
Young honeybee
Young one struggling for its place in the sun.

Guadeloupe
Searching
Searching itself
Searching will ensure the way.

Guadeloupe
Torment
Nocturnal torment
Torment growing keen despite the moon.

Guadeloupe
Object
Object waiting for judgement
Object moaning between hammer and anvil.

Guadeloupe
Chair
Sedan chair
Chair collapsing under the weight of passengers.

Guadeloupe
Rock
Angular rock
Rock supporting the secular building.

Guadeloupe
Horse
Sea horse
Horse struggling to reach land.

Guadeloupe
Messenger
Messenger of the night
Messenger bringing hope.

Guadeloupe
Good
Good fortune
Good news that tell some tall tales.

Jean Juraver
Guadeloupe

Dem People

Dem people a beautiful people
Hearing dem talk nice-nice story
All a dem want fuh lef' dem native boundary
Thinking dem go see so much glory.

Nough a dem a lef' dem country
Nough a dem a lef' dem family
You see deh queueing at de embassy
You see deh 'checking in' at de airport
Not forgetting the tips at de airline offices
Hoping to get reliable services.

As dem want a change in de white-man community
Deh mek use of all de opportunity
Some a dem a tek the right track
One-one a dem a get turn back
Having a desperate intention, just fuh go back.

D. H. Bhikhari
Guyana

Evergreen

I look towards the hills
Searching to find my will
It is time for change
It is time we mend our ways
like butterflies we flutter
from culture to culture
not taking time to nurture
that which is ours.

Strong hills covered with soft greens
towering with power and strength
So too we can be
rooted deep within this soil
rooted deep within this cause.

For a tree by itself is but a tree,
Many trees are a forest,
Why can't we be a forest
amongst others
together nurturing each other?

Rhonda Burnett
Trinidad and Tobago

No New Day Dawning

Tease my senses
And fill my mind
With the sounds of my land and people
Feed my eyes
And touch my heart
With the words of my kin and country

Were but all one and undivided
I would never fear
For my security would lie in
The place of my birth
And my resting place, in my heritage
—But my home is torn by the
    Claws of economics
    And beaten by those ignorant of
    Her lustre and beauty,
    Her brilliance and industry
    So they alone prosper.

Parasites! All of them!
Whose clothes reek of blood money
Whose abodes fume of evil ways
Whose wives the whore of Babylon can call sisters
Whose children are bastards of their concrete jungle.

... My opus is destroyed
    I am slowly invaded by enemies
    And my most treasured possession
    - my home -
    is no more.

Andra Browne-Schram
Trinidad and Tobago

Easter Song

Noon day blues
follows children down town
dancing in the sun
with fish bowl eyes
and pregnant smiles
arms stretched wide
for a few pieces of silver
rejection is a hole
deep in their pocket
these children bleed black
right there
on the street

Evening prayer:
eli eli lamma sabachthani
bow your head
in the sun children
roll inside your empty gut
sleep sweet like death
carried away
on that nightmare's
broad back
soon light
will slip
inside a corner
of the eye
force open the lid

morning crows
coughing dust
arise
from the earth children
weak like foetus
bush tea at the altar this morning
to build strength
for the sunday of your life
and when they come
for the rent

you are gone

Hugh Stultz
Britain/Jamaica

The Politician

As clear as mud he spoke
Pounding his fist to emphasize
the fraud of his ignorance,
like thunder
audience bang boards and desks
echoes of vibrating cheers
would cease at intervals
and pausing,
the speaker would ready himself to
launch more words of wisdom
to the unwise;
the hilarious act of gratitude
would increase again in
complexity
but soon perish in the momentum.
The man of the moment
gets up into higher gear,
words of approval
would boost the confidence
of this political puppet,
as this confidence climaxes
it would flow out unto the crowd
like unto the roar of a lion,
leaving them to react violently.
There was no way the proceeding
could be understood,
especially by people who are fairly educated,
people who know words and their meanings
people who know what it is like to be talented.
Hence the drama continued.
What if this man had collected?

No doubt support would be likewise
at full strength;
But blessed be him who sees money
as a deceiver,
denying himself of wealth
by giving away talent
to the charity of politics.

Norman Pottinger
Jamaica

Massacre in the Sun

A magically shimmering sky
Like the clearest diamond cut
On a blackened day.
Shimmering sky,
Mirage decorated sky,
On a blackened day.
A dream gone wrong.
Of promises returned to the dust,
The tricolour of false orders cuts the air
Where order sleeps in a sepulchre of horror
But yet to be blown on the wind
And stilled on a peasant disposition.
Daylight so crystal clear,
Banners which profuse the air
Like a sea enraged
On a mocking day.
See angered souls in the valley below.
Voices ring in defiance,
Salutes raised in triumph,
Guns loaded with urgency,
Ribbons cut in solemnity,
Medals worn with vanity,
While children grew in poverty.
In dictating cruelty each soul craved sanity.
Voices of order who legalised such a plight
Turning purest white into deathly red.
Reddened hands, reddened faces, reddened souls.
On a blackened day among golden sunshine.
Silence whenever it comes.
Bloody roses strewn to comfort man's grief
Black, brown and yellow — wherever placed,
We shared death's knell.

When my body's steeped in red,
I stare in awesome wonder at the sunlit purity of my land.
When I die,
I die among those massacred in the sun.

Kathleen Seenarine
Trindad and Tobago

Ruins

As I stood there
My eyes piercing through
that old dilapidated house

Near the edge of death
Soon ready to give off
Its last breath of life ...

It stood upon life's humble ground
Vines and leaves
growing through all open crevices

Its thatched roof
Ready to cave in
As if I sneezed in its presence
My thoughts would soon come to pass.

The old truck jammed against the front door
As though to give added support
before it came
to a sudden
down fall.

As I stood there
My mind wondering

as to how such a house could come
to such ruins

How did it occur?
No one knows

Why it is deserted?
I cannot say.

But —
this old wreckage

would
linger long
in
my mind.

Nicole De Coteau
Trinidad and Tobago

Returned at Last

Returned at last
To this short-spaced era
To find out only
That the grass does grow greener
On the other side.

Returned to bloated bellies
And shrunken eyeballs
And lips which can say nothing
Only the eyes cry for help.

Returned to roadside rumshops
And zombied vagrants counting days
And violated women counting sleepless nights
Feeling the earth slipping from under them.

Returned to a paradise
Not for the poor born into it
But for those who can afford
Where poverty sucks dry all hope
And chases away all dreams.

Returned at last
To what I never saw
In my sightless fall to the top
Yes, today I returned at last
To reality.

Yvette Regis
St. Lucia

NATURE

Mother Nature Makes Music

It came finally
Dispersing the dark atrocious clouds
Letting their components drop
Like quick silver
And it fell
With no reserve
Stripping the heat
Off the atmosphere

It came finally
Splashing and splattering
Filling the open buds
Of the roses
Drowning the lilies
And bathing the daisies
It ran off the pane
Like a melting ice cream

It came finally
Making music on the roof
A cataclysmic rhythm
Of drums, pans
Tambourine and cymbals
It made rock, reggae
Jazz and kaiso
They were all
Out of tune
The quartets and quavers
The sharps and flats
It was puzzling
It was annoying
It was sweet

I waited long
To hear the rhythm
I knew so well
To feel the rain's coolness
To hear its song

Ivenia Benjamin
Dominica

Rupununi, For her Lover the Rain

He will come in the stillness of the night
Creeping quietly lest I awake.
His wet fingers will caress me,
His misty lips will possess me,
He'll spread a cool blanket over me,
And in the comfort of his arms I'll be lost.

In my mind's warm room I waited for him
Knowing he'll keep his date.
For the flow of my thoughts depends on him,
He writes music for the songs I sing.
The peace of my soul is a gift from him,
And in his absence my body cries out.

I need him to cleanse my cluttered soul,
I need him to soothe my pain,
After heat's rough hands have frayed
The tender fibres of my cool,
Draining the moisture from my hopes,
And drying my pools of love.

Jacquie Prince
Guyana

For This One Night

Hold me close
through these lonely, darkened hours.
Hold me
and comfort me
and for a while
nothing can hurt me,
no pain can touch me
and my doubts can be locked
outside the security of your arms.

For this one night
embrace me,
let your flesh warm me
and your touch
spirit away my fears.
Let me close my eyes
knowing your strength is near to protect me.
Then come the morn'
We'll pull the curtains,
let the daylight in
and I can begin my day knowing
that for one night,
I was safe
and come the 'morrow,
I am still whole.

Michelle Molyneux
Britain

My Leguan Beauty

Me never see one beauty like she,
Rani ah me dream!
She ah everything me ever want in Leguan,
Rani ah the one and only beauty in Guyana
Who can make my heart beat like tassa drum.

She na know da,
Rani na know me love her so!
Rani ah the only one in my life,
She make me foot go weak like coconut jelly.

Rani ah me dream!
Rani only ah fantasy,
She belong to another,
She brock me heart!
Only me know the pain of a love
for a millionaire's daughter.

She the only one who can hurt me,
She the only one who can cause the pain,
She my love,
She never give me a second glance,
She never will because me ah she father labourer!
He ah me bass!
Nevermind she ah me sunshine and rain,
She what I'm living for in vain.

Rani's like a Kamal Gata flower
That grows in the seven pond ah the Botanical Garden,
She pure full of dew and fun,
She belong to ah millionaire!
She only ah fantasy to ah poor labourer,
Who never exist for her.

Saveeta Seenauth
Guyana

Tall Ebony

Cluttered, curly, carefree hair,
Danced above her mahogany skin,
Wood so sure of a face so pure,
But the sun refused to go in.

Springing hands,
Containing no bands,
Of gold to match her smile,
While cloistered curls and dress's swirls,
Angered the sun to a sin.

The magic feet that peeped tall ebony,
That dusted the ground with stars
Gave ample time to walk sublime,
In the sunlight's pure trace -
Who in jealousy retired — disgraced.

Aminatta Kamara
Britain

Sleep
(to my Mother)

moonlight hits the window
the wind sings a mournful
lullaby, trees take on
a different shape

as i pass by the window
i see dreams of peacocks,
wonders one has never
seen, fly quickly

for the child stirs
— we find comfort in
our mother's arms —

outside is cold and
windy
but you are
warm with love

for a moment i
pause to think
of the warm night
i used to know

then it is time to take
back my old shape
an old tree with a tear
running from my branch

think i have the
sunlight of the
morrow to warm me

Maya Matthews
Britain/St. Lucia/Guyana

Date With An Angel

Last night
Like the sunrise
It dawned on me
Like a curious child
I stood
      Gaping
With wide eyes
I beheld it
Falling from the skies
Bright and intense
Like diamonds formed in the earth's womb
It stole my fascination
Belittled all I imagined
The angel of experience
Floating on the clouds
Then riding on the waves
      Experiences of joys
        Experiences of pains
          Loving experiences
            Memorable experiences
Their provider goes away
But will come back
Even as memories
      That grow old and never die
I know that you will come back
Sweet angel of experience
You will always hold my fascination
And be the inspiration
      Of my imagined things.

Yvette Regis
St. Lucia

Eclaircie

Soleil de tes yeux.
Lumière du centre de ta terre.
Ton nez comme un carbet se perd
Dans la source de ta bouche
Où apparaît de temps en temps
L'écume de tes dents.
Eternel mouvement tirant sur
Les collines de tes joues
Qui se teintent selon
Le temps que fait ton front.
Tremblement de ta peau
Raz de marée de ton sang
Anticyclone ou dépression de tes pores.
Ton visage se bouleverse
Au rythme des acalmies et des intempéries.
A le regarder ainsi
Il mélange les couleurs
Et change ses expressions
Comme l'anoli sur la branche
Posant pour on ne sait quel peintre
Qui lui donnera l'éternité.

Allix Belrose-Huyghues
Germany/Guadeloupe/Martinique

A Break in the Clouds

Sun from your eyes.
Light from the centre of your earth.
Your nose, like a jetty, loses itself
In the gulf of your mouth
Where, from time to time, appears
The foam of your teeth.
Eternal movement pulling on
the hills of your cheeks
Which blush according to
The weather of your brow
Quaking of your skin
Tide-wave of your blood
Anti-cyclone or depression of your pores.
Your face somersaults
To the rhythm of fidgets and malcontents.
Seen thus,
It mixes colours
And changes their expressions
Like the anoli on the branch
Posing for any old artist
Who will give it eternity.

Allix Belrose-Huyghues
Germany/Guadeloupe/Martinique

SOCIETY

A Poem

Awake ...
because I am,
and stumble through a door
into a world devoid of guile,
existent
beyond men's comprehension
and nurtured by his ...
Dreams ...
because I sleep,
if only to awake
in sight out of mind
and see our twisted ideologies
locked, in conflict
dancing upon the bones of religion,
and chained to the pillars of mis-conception
and ...
Awake
because I sleep,
and see this world which yawns before me,
engulfing my reality ...
Asleep.

Glen Rampersad
Trinidad and Tobago

Waiting

From the time you born
It have a routine
To be followed.
Everything
All Man's conflicts
His destruction of lives
Is just distraction
From the waiting.
Friends die — that hurts —
Big wake and people crying.
That does take up some time
But dry season pass
Rainy season come
You back in the same waiting.
Life's humour, fear, is nothing,
Like when you bounce up old pardners,
Liming on the street,
And they buff you up
And everybody feeling good,
Or when they say
Rastas break in next door
And t'ief de people things
And beat up de old man
And you say
Oh Lord
What if dat did happen to me,
You see all a dat
That is just for passing time
Just to alleviate the waiting.
But then, finally
You expect it
You say it reaching
And you anxious,
Like for Sparrow next tune

Or for Minshall band
And you say this is it
Look,
It coming now
Right here
And ...
And it don't appear.
Then we back into waiting,
Just waiting.
But hear nah, is what we waiting for?
Is for God
Or Jah, Allah
For it, or for whatever?
And I bet you, even with death
You go be still waiting
Just waiting,
Waiting ...

Edward C. Neehall
Trinidad and Tobago

Papa Struggle

From morning till nite
In sun and rain, he got fo go.
Poor Papa, me cry for him plenty nite.

Wah me can do?
Me can't do nothing,
nothing at all!
Papa got fo work hard to mind us.

De time so hard now,
And thing na cheap!
If Papa na work one day abie starve.
God bless him,
God bless Papa!

When you see he eye open morning,
Hmm! him got fo graze him cows,
Na matta what kind of weather.
You see him come home tired,
Sweat ah run down he skin;
balancing da bundle grass on his head.

Him work na done!
He got fo milk da cow and walk,
Yes walk! and sell da milk.
People cuss him, he na deserve it!
Not from you and not from me.

Papa na deserve one hurtful word,
Not from you, not from nobody.
So you see him plant his farm,
An a-graze his cows!
if him na do da abie starve.

God bless Papa.
In sun and rain,
Thunder,
Lightning,
Storm,
No matta what kind of weather,
He has to work.

People na know only abie know!
Yea! abie know how he got for struggle.
Just to give one daily bread to his family,
and give his pickney little education
cause Papa got no education.

He na deserve one hutfull word,
Yes! not from you, not from me,
Not from the world.
God Bless Papa his struggle is over.

Saveeta Seenauth
Guyana

A Strange Life Story

Poor old soul
takes up his pick-axe
and strikes with all his might.
Slowly raising his head
He takes up the axe, strikes again
then crumbles to the earth with a bang.

From the side walk
       I too
watch him groan in pain.
His wrinkled face squashes
as it surrenders stout-heartedly to the unknown.

The palm of his hands
scratches the ground
and finally clinches
the last feel of life thereon.

And with eyes pulping
and tongue outstretched,
the aged body trembles
and comes to a stand still.

In silence
all watch the bitter scene,
searching the blankness of others' faces
for answers.

And with shameful pride
I move on,
turning my back on memory,
leaving death and hell for a new page in History.

Norman Pottinger
Jamaica

71

Innocent and Guilty

We are the product of our society
We set the wheel in motion
and lubricate it to run smoothly
Great contributions indeed we've made
For this we do to the best of our ability
We're never appreciated or respected
and are kept in the background and the shade
While the leeches and ticks
Are paid handsomely
and honoured for their deceitful inhuman tactics
They walk through and upon us
They'll never walk with us
They look upon us not as their people,
but as their things.
Buying and selling us over and over again
They've only removed the shackles, chains and the rings
For only by controlling our minds can they secure their
gain
The best among us are taken to serve their numerous
desires
Our men of vision either rot in jail or slain
So-called leaders are handpicked by them
and controlled by wires
I often hear my people call on God
to relieve their suffering and pain
The God they've shown was produced by their
psychologist,
Their God is a mist, once blinded one cannot resist.
No crime have we committed
Yet we've always been convicted
We are the Innocent, you are the Guilty

When our turn comes we'll have no pity
From the depths we'll arise and destroy your abominable
city
It's a slow but irreversible phenomena
Victory is ours, Mr Slave Master
For your Guilt shall be your executioner.

Fabian La Roche
Trinidad and Tobago

A Society Logic/A Logic Society

A Society Logic

Stamp out ignorance and lack of charity.
Kick the human race into touch.
Lash out to be heard.
Drown hate and injustice.
Shoot out against false imprisonment.

A Logic Society

War creates peacemakers?
War creates peace?
War creates peace of mind?
War creates a few more things,
         death, death, death, death ...

Gloria Knowles
Britain

Caribbean Death

I tried examining my heart once
and instead of ignorant bliss
and blissful ignorance
I felt an organ pulsating
with hatred
throbbing with bitterness
I felt an organ
through which blood flowed incessantly
green with envy
for those who had brought
abused and rejected me.
I felt an organ
cold hard and necessary
to my existence.

I ponder now
the weakness of my acceptance
my rights to a black man's heart
and my arrival centuries ago
from across an ocean;
For I am no longer who I was
and who I was I can no longer be
My heart is soiled and my red blood
no longer vital.

Bonnie Peters
Trinidad and Tobago

Qui Etre

QUI ETRE
S'écrie René Depestre,
En sommant l'être humain
Où qu'il se trouve,
En ces temps de feu et de sang,
De répondre à cette question,
Et de recycler ses identitées singulières,
Régionales ou nationales
Dans le courant principal
De l'évolution du monde,
Pour une identité panhumaine.

Je suis
De tous les continents
Une femme qui marche
A travers les temps.
Je n'ai ni couleurs, ni appartenances, ni origines.
Je suis
De toutes les couleurs et de toutes les origines.
Je me tiens
Au croisement de tous les continents,
Et je tisse
Une poésie,
Celle de L'humanité réunie
En accord avec sa NATURE ...

Allix Belrose-Huyghues
Germany/Guadeloupe/Martinique

Who To Be

WHO TO BE?
Exclaims René Depestre,
Calling on human beings,
Wherever they are,
In these times of fire and blood,
To answer this question
And to recycle their separate identities,
Regional or national
In the mainstream
Of world evolution,
For panhuman identity.

I am
Of all continents.
A woman who walks
Across time.
I have neither colours, nor belongings, nor origins.
I am
Of all colours and all origins.
I stand
At the crossroads of all continents,
And I weave
A poetry,
That of reunited humanity
In harmony with its NATURE ...

Allix Belrose-Huyghues
Germany/Guadeloupe/Martinique

BEING

My Special Friends

You filled my childhood days
With wonders and adventures
You taught me so many things
Your knowledge was infinite

You told me things I never knew
You took me places I'd never been
You showed me things I'd never seen
You fed me food I'd never eaten

You are my constant companions
You never grew tired of my questions
You helped me thru' my examinations
And now some of you are in deterioration

You bring laughter to my voice
And sometimes you make me very sad
With your tales of broken-heart and woe
                    and death
But for all the world
I would not give you up —
My special collection of books.

Jean Harripersaud
Guyana

Pierrot et Colombine

Ne riez surtout pas des amours enfantines,
De ces sentiments purs,
Dénudés, sans parure,
De ces baisers d'enfants
Si doux et si touchants.

Non! Ne vous moquez pas, laissez-donc Colombine
Sourire à son Pierrot!
Voyez, ils sont si beaux...

Quelquefois je regarde en ce coin de mon coeur,
Cet endroit où demeure un peu de mon enfance.
Alors pour moi le temps interrompt sa cadence
Et je revis les jours pastels de mon bonheur.

Ne riez pas! J'ai eu des amours enfantines.
C'étaient bonbons volés
Aussitôt partagés,
Courses dans la rosée,
Rendez-vous sous l'ondée.

Dans un bal costumé, j'ai pu, en Colombine,
Embrasser mon Pierrot.
Ses yeux étaient si beaux...

Franciane Valétudie
Guadeloupe

Pierrot and Colombine

Whatever you do, don't laugh at childhood love,
These pure sentiments,
Naked, unadorned
These children's kisses
So tender and so touching.

No! Don't sneer. Let Colombine
Smile on her Pierrot.
Look, they're so sweet ...

Sometimes I peer into this nook of my heart,
This spot where a little of my childhood dwells.
Thus, for me, Time interrupts his flow
And I relive my pastel days of happiness.

Don't laugh! I had childhood loves.
They were stolen sweets
Impulsively shared,
Visits to the rose-arbour
Assignations under the water-fall.

Disguised as Colombine, I could kiss my Pierrot
In masquerade,
His eyes were so lovely ...

Franciane Valétudie
Guadeloupe

On Being Apart

Dearest brother
How yuh do
Is ah long time
Me naw see yuh
Me miss yuh
Remember the times
When we played
"Hoto Motto"
"Go an smell de didi"
Remember when dad did ketch us
They were really really
Funny times

Plantain, beans and egg
A mountain of bread
Bread and butter pudding
Bwoy, you could really eat

Always there
the memories we hold
When we remember
We hug ourselves
And smile
And laugh
And cry

We grow
Sometimes to part
We are always linked
Parting can never be for
Too long
SOON
We will all be together again
Again embraces, hugs, kisses
Even tears

LOVE

Despite the length of time
The distance
The silence

ISOLATION

We all feel it
Always there is the love
Forever hold that thought
Much love to you
And my dear niece
I am your sister

Jay A. James
Britain

Lost for Words

My mind goes blank, sometimes
and I'm lost for words.
I want to write, a novel,
a book, just a journal entry
or maybe a poem.

Not a thought in my mind,
nothing felt in the heart
Pen in hand, with the
paper staring me dead in the face,
Empty with so much desire.

Wanting to say so much
Needing to express myself, beyond time
needing to create,
And I find myself
Lost, lost for words.

Carlos A. Permell
Britain

Much Much More

It is much
much more
than can be seen on the surface,
but pain limits its form,
expression
and gesture.
So just hold me;
let the music become the earth
as we feast upon insecurity
brushed aside
for one instant,
or an aeon.

It is much
much more
than can be touched or felt,
but can be sensed
in the darkness of want,
silence
and vulnerability.
So just accept
With no explanation;
understand
without justification.

It is so much more
than you can ever know.
It is much much more.

Michelle Molyneux
Britain

Glossary

N.B. The translations of the French poems into English do not set out to have the same artistic value as the French originals.

Abi (abie): Guyanese Creole word meaning everybody.

Abiku: in Nigeria an evil spirit or spirit of the unborn which prevents women giving natural birth.

Allah: Muslim name for God.

Amon: Ancient Egyptian Ram-headed God.

Amon-Ra: Assimilation of the ancient Egyptian gods Amon and Ra to avoid rivalry between both gods.

Anoli: small green lizard.

Arawaks: one of the groups of Amerindians to be the first inhabitants of the Caribbean.

Assalaam-Au-Alaikum: Muslim greeting meaning 'Peace be unto you'.

Babylon: country named in the Bible, used by Rastafarians to symbolise the oppression of the Western World.

bass: Creole for boss

buff (boof): to insult in jest.

bwoy: Creole for boy.

Caribs: one of the groups of Amerindians to be the first inhabitants of the Caribbean.

Chac-chac: musical instrument made from a dried gourd and seeds.

Colombine: a French pantomime character especially popular during Carnival time and often Pierrot's partner.

Congo: African drum

coolie: derogatory name for East Indians living in the Caribbean.

Crick...Crack: phrase used to introduce and end a story — used in the story telling tradition from West Africa.

cuss: 'curse' — meaning to swear.

Derek Walcott: Caribbean poet from St. Lucia

Douens (duennes): Trinidadian folk characters — the spirits of children who died before being baptised.

Eli eli lamma sabachthani: words spoken by Jesus on the cross meaning: 'My God, my God why hast thou forsaken me'.

Go an smell de didi: game invented by the author.

Horus: the falcon-headed sun god of Memphis in Egypt.

Hospikal: Jamaican Creole word for hospital.

Hoto Moto: game invented by the author.

I & I: Rastafarian expression meaning I or me.

Isis: the mother goddess in ancient Egypt.

Jah: Rastafarian word used especially in prayer when referring to Emperor Haile Selassie as God.

Kaiso (calypso, cariso): original slave song based on social, political issues; most popular around Carnival time especially in Trinidad.

Kamal Ghata Flower: lotus lily — Victoria Regia.

Khem: Ancient Egyptian civilisation — the word Khem meaning black and referring to the skin colour of the people.
Lagahou (ligahoo): Trinidadian folk character, often an old man who can change into a vicious animal, lay curses, protect nature, etc.
Lambi: conch shell used to summon people by blowing through it.
La Rose: traditional folk festival in St. Lucia.
Laventille: urban area in Port of Spain Trinidad — birth-place of the steel band.
Leguan: island on the Essequibo River in Guyana. The island is inhabited.
liming: Trinidadian word meaning getting together with friends.
locks: term used by Rastafarians to describe their hair that is never cut and therefore left to grow into natural locks.
Minshall: Peter Minshall, popular Trinidadian designer of Carnival costumes/band leader.
Natty: tightly curled African hair.
Orni: head covering worn by Muslim women.
Osiris: the king and judge of the dead in ancient Egypt.
Paddy-fields: rice fields.
Papa Bois: widely known Trinidadian folk character — the Old Man of the Woods. He is the guardian of the animals and the custodian of the trees.
pardners: partners; male friends.
pickney: 'English' Creole word meaning child/children.
Pierrot: a French pantomime character especially popular during Carnival time and often the partner of Colombine.
Pitons: high pointed mountains in St. Lucia renowned for their beauty.
plantain: family to the banana but eaten only when cooked.
Ra: Ancient Egyptian Sun god.
Rasta: shortened version for Rastafari (the name of the Emperor Haile Selassie), a popular religion in Jamaica and throughout the Caribbean.
René Depestre: Haitian novelist.
Rupununi: region of Guyana.
Shabine: person of mixed race (African and European) light-skinned and with light-coloured, curly hair.
Shalwal: trousers worn by Muslim women.
Shango: West African God of Thunder and Lightning; an African based religion in parts of the Caribbean.
Sheba: Black biblical queen.
Sitar: Indian stringed musical instrument.
Sparrow: stage name of famous Trinidadian calypsonian, Slinger Francisco.
Sulphur Springs: volcanic sulphur springs in St. Lucia said to have healing properties.
t'ief: thief (the 'h' is not pronounced in Creole).
Trinity: (Trinidad). Columbus named the island after seeing the three hills in South Trinidad.
Yam: West African/Caribbean root vegetable.